TOTALLY AWESOME PARACORD CRAFTS

Are you ready to make some amazingly cool projects with paracord? It's *knot* hard! This book is loaded with tips, tricks, and designs you can use to make some totally awesome stuff. Whether it's a bold bracelet or wraps that rock, there's a ton of fun to be found on these pages. This book is not just about bracelets (although there are lots of those, too!). There are some totally off-the-wall projects for you to try—like paracord figures (page 46) and even a dreamcatcher (page 50)! If you really want a challenge, check out the Monkey's Fist Keychain (page 54). As you work through the projects, be sure to keep an eye out for all kinds of ways to mix up the designs and make them your own, like choosing a color scheme based on your favorite superhero or sports team. Are you excited yet? Let's get started!

Look what you can make!

Go crazy with paracord!

Projects

20

Cobra Stitch Bracelet

30

Fishtail Bracelet

46

Building Block Bob

Cobra Colors Bracelet **26**

Totally Triple Bracelet **34**

Loopy Lanyard or Necklace **38**

Rockin' Wraps **42**

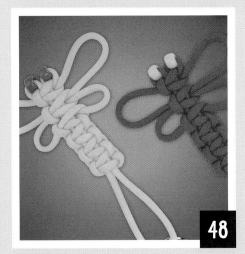

Darting Dragonfly **48**

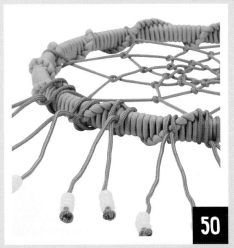

Dreamcatcher **50**

Monkey's Fist Keychain **54**

Knot it, Wrap it... Rock it!

4

Fun
with
friends!

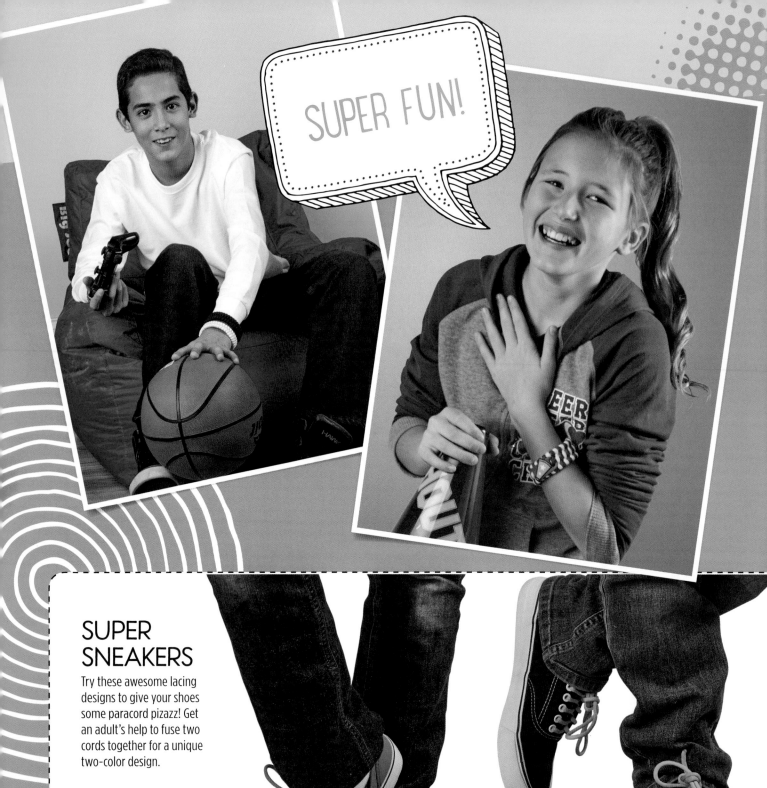

SUPER FUN!

SUPER SNEAKERS

Try these awesome lacing designs to give your shoes some paracord pizazz! Get an adult's help to fuse two cords together for a unique two-color design.

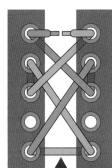

CRISS CROSS

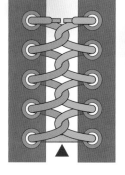

ZIPPER

ZIGZAG

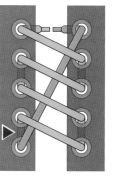

SINGLE BAR

STARBURST

PARACORD

Ready to get started? First, let's expand your paracord knowledge! Read through this section to learn some interesting facts about paracord, and some tips and tricks for working with it. Once you're finished here, turn to page 14 to start tying some knots!

TOOLS AND MATERIALS

Paracord. Did you know that paracord is short for parachute cord? It got the name because it was first used by the army for lines on parachutes, so you know it's super strong. Paracord comes in thick, thin, and super-thin sizes (you will see these labeled as 550, 325, and 95 at the craft store). Paracord also comes in tons of awesome colors, including reflective and glow-in-the-dark. The materials list for each project will tell you how much cord you will need, and in what colors!

Scissors. You can't cut your paracord without scissors! Make sure you have a nice pair that cut well. Dull scissors will leave your cord ends frayed.

Yardstick or tape measure. You'll need several feet of paracord for each project, so something longer than a regular ruler will make measuring extra easy.

Grill lighter. ❗ Don't use this without an adult's help.

Glue. Use this to finish cord ends to prevent fraying.

Jigs. If you see loads of bracelets in your future, you might want to pick up a jig from your local craft store (or turn to page 10 to learn how to make your own). By using a jig, you'll be able to whip up bracelets in no time at all. You can also purchase jigs for making monkey's fist knots.

Beads, buckles, and accessories. There are loads of ways to make your paracord creations stand out. You can use different colors and sizes of buckles for bracelets and all kinds of beads, charms, rings, and other accessories to really make them your own.

THE PERFECT SIZE

Paracord comes in three different sizes: 550 (thick), 325 (thin), and 95 (super-thin). You can use any size you want for the projects in this book, but your finished project may just look a little different depending on which you use. A bracelet made with 325 cord will be thinner than a bracelet made with 550 cord. Also, you will have to make more knots if you use thin or super-thin cord.

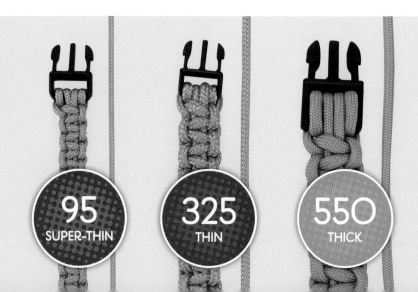

95 SUPER-THIN **325** THIN **550** THICK

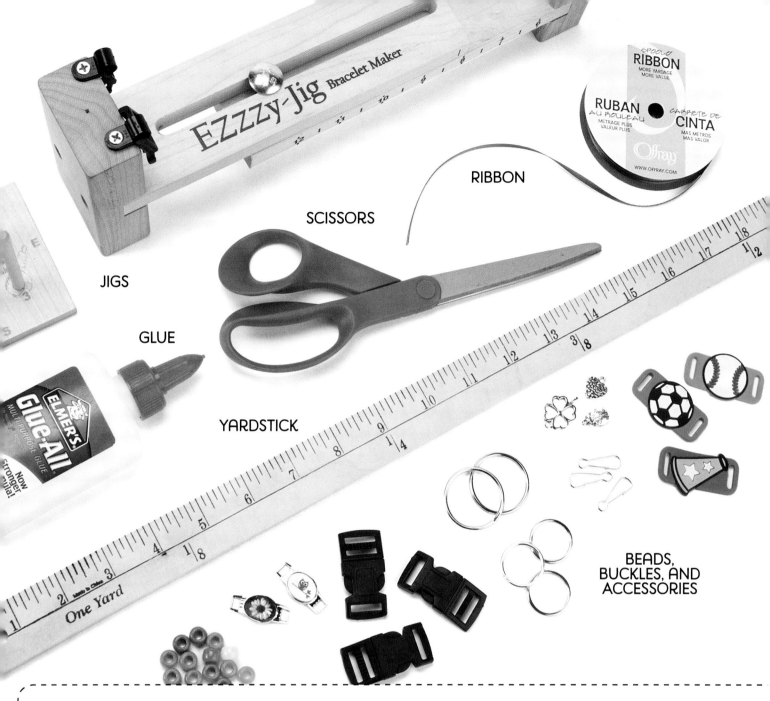

RIBBON

SCISSORS

JIGS

GLUE

YARDSTICK

BEADS, BUCKLES, AND ACCESSORIES

CREATIVE COLORS

Paracord comes in so many different colors, there are tons of ways you can use them to represent some of your favorite things. Try making a bracelet using the colors of your favorite sports team or superhero. What about the colors of your school? If you wanted to make a princess bracelet, what colors would you pick? What colors would you use for a bracelet based on a video game character? Check out the edges of the pages as you work through this book for some totally awesome color combos. Which one do you like best?

Shown here are: Rainbow, Glow in the Dark, White, Titanium, Army Camo, Gray, Reflective Black, Black, Purple, Navy, Royal Blue, Turquoise, Olive Drab, Kelly Green, Neon Green, Yellow, Neon Yellow, Gold, Reflective Orange, Neon Orange, Red, Neon Pink, Light Pink, Pink Camo, Maroon, Desert Camo.

TIPS & TRICKS

REMOVING FILLER
Paracord is made of an outer jacket (the colorful part) that's braided around filler strands (these are white). You can take the filler out of the paracord before starting a project, or you can leave it in. Removing the filler will make the cord flatter, which will make your knots flatter, too! Here's how to take out the filler.

1 Cut off both ends of the cord. Tap your finger on the cord ends until the filler strands get very frayed and fluffy.

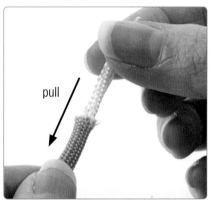

pull

2 Grab the filler strands with one hand and hold on to them. With your other hand, slide the jacket down the filler strands and off the other end.

TIP
Make sure you slide the jacket off the filler strands. Don't try to pull the filler strands out of the jacket.

USING A JIG
Using a jig can help you make bracelets super fast. And it's easy! Here's how.

1 Your jig will have a buckle end on each side. This one even has two buckle sizes! Take the buckle ends you are using for your bracelet and clip them onto the jig's buckle ends.

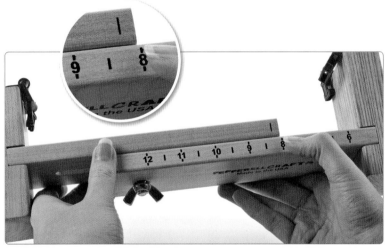

2 Adjust the jig to the measurement you want for your finished bracelet. All the bracelets in this book are made to be just a little longer than 8" (20.5cm), with knotted sections about 6½" (16.5cm) long. See page 11 for tips on calculating the length of your bracelet.

Making your own jig is as easy as gluing two blocks of wood to each end of a board. Attach a buckle end to each block. For the jig shown, the buckles were attached using screws and wrapping knots (page 19). Search online for loads of homemade jig ideas.

STARTING A BRACELET

Almost all of the bracelets in this book can be started using the following steps. Don't worry if you forget how to do this, because each individual project will give you steps for setting up your bracelet. But if you want to practice, you can always come back to this section!

1 Tie the cord onto a buckle end using a lark's head or double lark's head knot (page 14). To do this, fold the cord in half to form a loop at the center. Feed the cord ends up through a buckle end, then bring the cord ends down through the loop (lark's head). Feed the cord ends up through the buckle and down through the loop again (double lark's head).

2 Bring the cord ends down through the other buckle end. You can wrap each cord around the buckle twice to fill up the space. Position the buckle ends so they are about 6½" (16.5cm) apart.

3 There will be two cords that stretch between your buckle ends. These are the filler cords. There will be two loose cords. These are your working cords.

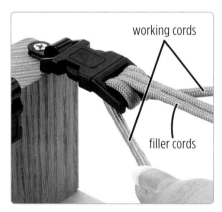

working cords

filler cords

FINDING THE PERFECT LENGTH

All the bracelets in this book are made to be just a little longer than 8" (20.5cm), with knotted sections about 6½" (16.5cm) long. But you might need a size that's a little bit bigger or smaller. Let's figure out how long you should make a bracelet to fit your wrist. Take your buckle and close it. Measure how long the closed buckle is. Now, measure around your wrist. Take your wrist measurement and subtract the buckle measurement. Add ½" (1.5cm) to your answer. Paracord can be a bit stiff, so adding a little extra wiggle room is a good idea.

HERE'S AN EXAMPLE:

Let's say your buckle is...

1½" (4CM) LONG

...and your wrist measures...

6" (15CM) AROUND

Subtract the buckle measurement from your wrist measurement...

6" – 1½" = 4½"
(15CM – 4CM = 11CM)

Add ½" (1.5cm) to your answer...

4½" + ½" = 5"
(11CM + 1.5CM = 12.5CM)

Make the knotted portion of your bracelet...

5" (12.5CM) LONG!

TRY THESE VIDEO GAME CHARACTER COLOR PAIRS: Can you guess the characters from their colors?

6½" (16.5cm)

FINISHING ENDS: GLUE

Paracord is made of many small strands of nylon braided together. When you cut the end of a cord, the braid will begin to unravel and the cord end will become frayed. You can keep this from happening by using everyday white multi-purpose glue to finish your cord ends.

JOINING CORDS

To join two colors of cord, you will need to use super glue or the fusing technique on page 13. Make sure you ask for an adult's help if fusing cord.

FINISHING ENDS

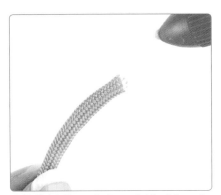

1 To finish the end of a cord, trim it to make it as even as possible. Then, cover the end with glue. Be sure to cover both the white filler and the outer colored casing. As the glue dries and becomes tacky, you can shape the end of the cord with your fingers.

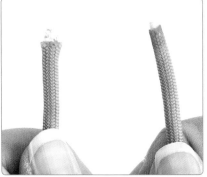

2 Once the glue has dried, the end of the cord should be slightly hard and stiff like the cord on the right, making it easier to thread through buckle ends or beads. Unfinished cord ends will fray, like the cord on the left.

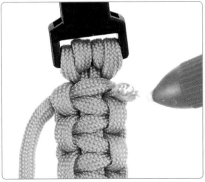

3 To finish a project with glue, trim the cord ends as close to the project as possible. Then, completely cover the cord ends with glue. This will secure them on your project and keep them from fraying.

DID YOU KNOW?

Paracord has tons of uses, even in computers! Joe Mercado uses paracord to sleeve his custom cables for modified computer cases like the one shown at the right. Learn more at *modders-inc.com*.

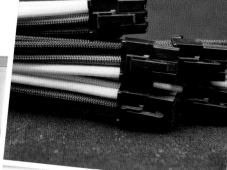

Courtesy of Dewayne Carel (left) and Joe Mercado (right), *modders-inc.com*.

FUSING CORD

Parents, this section is for you! Paracord is made out of nylon, which will melt under heat. Instead of using glue, you can use heat to finish the ends of cords and prevent fraying. You can also join cords that are two different colors together. If your child would like to fuse paracord, he or she will need your help.

FINISHING ENDS

1 To finish the end of a cord, hold the flame of a grill lighter near, but not on, the end of the cord. This will soften and melt the cord so it can be shaped. Make sure you do not put the cord in the flame; this will burn and blacken it.

2 Once the end of the cord is softened, shape it using the side of your scissors.

HERE'S YOUR SIGN!

Always help your child when you see this symbol ❗ on the photo for a project.

JOINING CORDS

1 Join two cords together by holding the cords side by side with the ends even. Hold the flame of a grill lighter near the ends of the cord to soften and melt them at the same time.

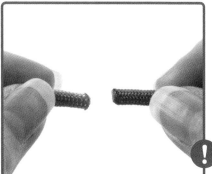

2 Take the bottom cord and turn it so the ends of the two cords are facing one another. Push the ends together and hold them in place until they cool. Do this quickly or the cord ends will cool and harden before they can be pushed together.

3 Hold the flame of a grill lighter near the spot where the cords are joined. Spin the cord in your fingers to heat all sides. Smooth and shape the softened area where the cords are joined with the side of your scissors.

DON'T TOUCH!

Melted paracord is very hot. Make sure you or your child never touch the fused ends of cord with your fingers.
Use the side of a pair of scissors to shape the cord as needed.

You only need to learn a few knots to make the projects in this book. Some knots might seem hard at first, but they are very repetitive, so be patient and keep working. You'll master them in no time. And once you get the hang of it, you'll be making loads of projects!

LARK'S HEAD KNOT

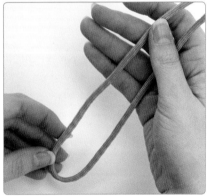

1 Fold the cord in half. This will form a loop at the center. Hold on to the center loop.

2 Place the center loop under the item you're attaching the cord to (like the buckle for a bracelet).

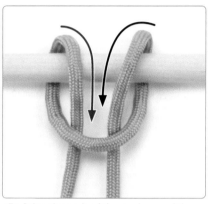

3 Bring the ends of the cord around the item and down through the center loop. Pull tight, and the cord will be snugly attached to your item.

DOUBLE LARK'S HEAD KNOT

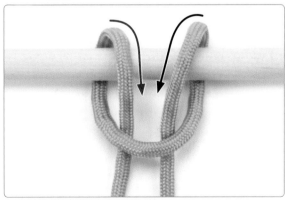

1 Make a lark's head knot following the steps above.

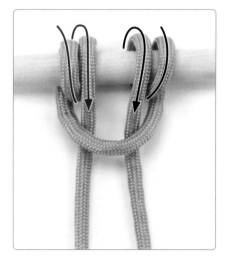

2 Now bring the ends of the cord around the item you're attaching the cord to and down through the center loop again, just like you did to make the lark's head knot.

HALF HITCH KNOT

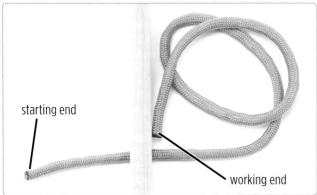

starting end

working end

1 Place one end of your cord under the item you are wrapping (like a pencil or flashlight). This is the starting end. The remaining long end is the working end.

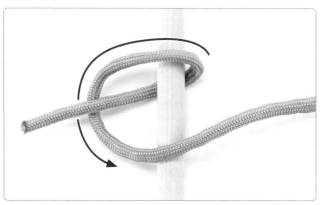

2 Bring the long working end of the cord around the short starting end. This will form a loop around the item you are wrapping.

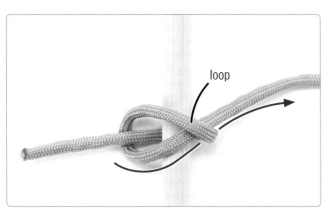

loop

3 Bring the working end through the loop you made in Step 2.

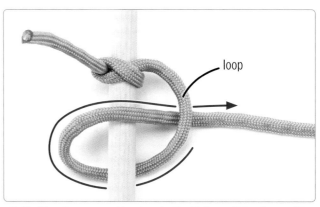

loop

4 You'll make your next knot under the first one. Bring the working end around the item you are wrapping to start forming a loop. Feed the working end of the cord through the loop to finish it. Tighten the loop.

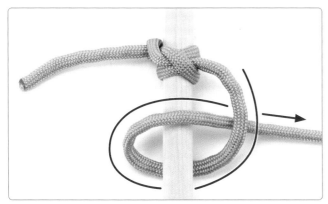

5 Repeat Step 4, bringing the working end around the item you are wrapping and feeding it through the loop that forms.

6 This is what the half hitch looks like when you repeat it.

SQUARE KNOT

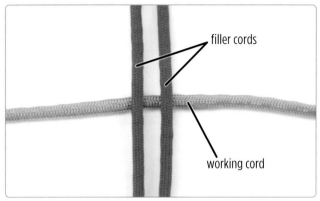

filler cords

working cord

1 In this book, you will always make your square knots over filler cords. To start, take two filler cords (orange) and place them side by side. Take the cord you will tie the knots with (this is called the working cord, shown in blue) and place it under the filler cords, making a plus sign as shown.

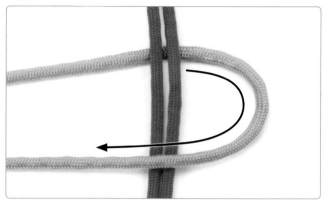

2 Bring the right working cord over the filler cords.

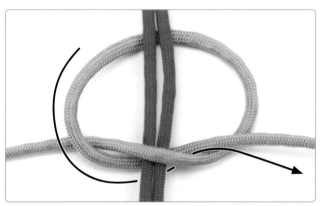

3 Bring the left working cord over the right working cord, under the filler cords, and over and through the loop formed by the right working cord.

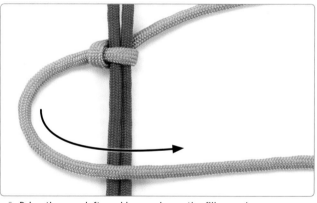

4 Bring the new left working cord over the filler cords.

TIP

This knot is a lot like the one you use to start tying your shoes, except you are tying it around filler cords!

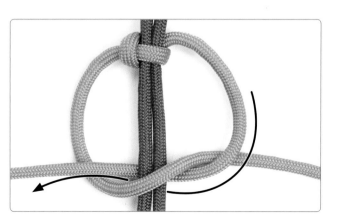

5 Bring the right working cord over the left working cord, under the filler cords, and over and through the loop formed by the left working cord.

SQUARE KNOT STRIPE

1 Take two filler cords (orange) and place them side by side. Remove the filler from the cord you'd like to use for the stripe (see page 10) and place the stripe cord (green) between the filler cords. Take the cord you will tie the knots with (this is called the working cord, shown in blue) and place it under the filler and stripe cords, making a plus sign as shown.

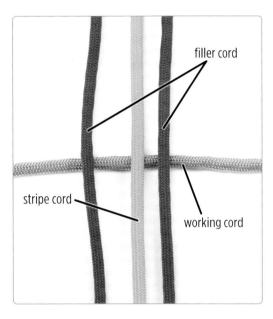

filler cord

stripe cord

working cord

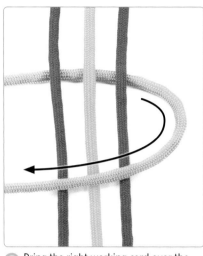

2 Bring the right working cord over the filler and stripe cords.

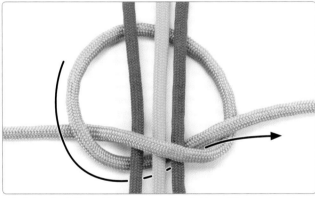

3 Bring the left working cord over the right working cord, under the filler and stripe cords, and over and through the loop formed by the right working cord.

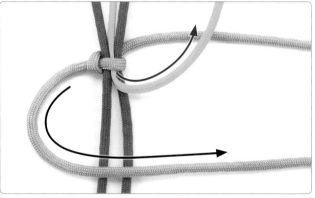

4 You will tie the next part of the knot under the stripe cord. To do this, flip the stripe cord beneath the first knot up out of the way. Then, bring the left working cord over the filler cords.

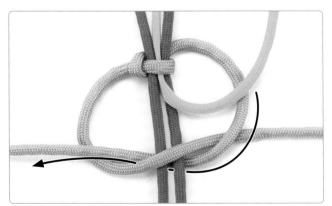

5 Bring the right working cord over the left working cord, under the filler cords, and over the through the loop formed by the left working cord.

6 Flip the stripe cord back down on top of the filler cords and repeat Steps 2–3 to tie a knot over the filler and stripe cords. Then, repeat Steps 4–5 to tie a knot under the stripe cord as shown. Continue repeating this over-under pattern.

ROUND BRAID

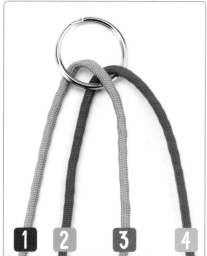

1 Fold two cords in half over the item you are braiding onto (like a key ring). Make sure the colors alternate. See how the pattern is blue, orange, blue, orange?

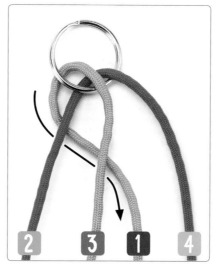

2 Bring the far left strand under the two strands in the middle. Shown here, the far left blue strand (1) goes under the orange and blue strands (2 and 3) in the middle.

3 Now bring the strand you are braiding with back over one strand to the left. Shown here, the blue strand (1) that you moved in Step 2 goes back over the blue strand (3), to the left.

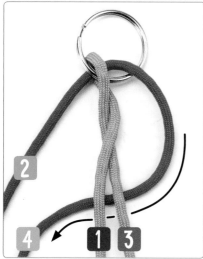

4 Now you are going to repeat the pattern on the right side. Bring the far right strand under the two strands in the middle. Shown here, the far right orange strand (4) goes under the two blue strands (1 and 3) in the middle.

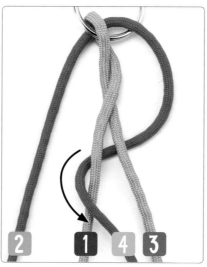

5 Now bring the strand you are braiding with back over one strand to the right. Shown here, the orange strand (4) that you moved in Step 4 goes back over the blue strand (1), to the right.

6 Continue the pattern, by repeating Steps 2–5.

TIP   In Step 1, try arranging the cords so the strands of the same color are side by side (blue, blue, orange, orange). This will make straight vertical stripes in the finished braid.

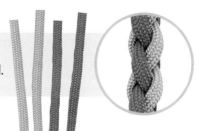

WRAPPING KNOT

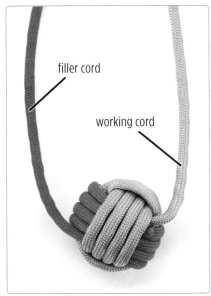

filler cord

working cord

1 This is the perfect way to finish the Monkey's Fist Keychain on page 54. When you start, you will have two cord ends. The left cord (orange) will be the filler cord and the right cord (blue) will be the working cord.

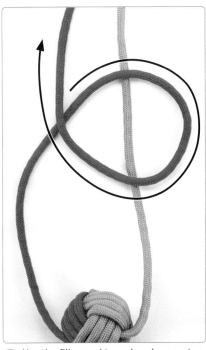

2 Use the filler cord to make a loop on top of the working cord.

3 Pinch all the cords together at the center of the loop.

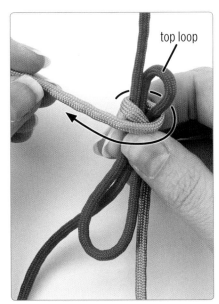

top loop

4 Take the working cord (blue) and wrap it around all the cords you are pinching together. Leave a little bit of the top of the loop sticking out past the working cord.

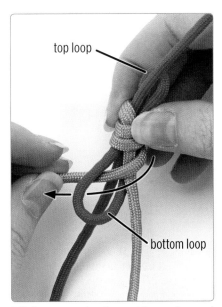

top loop

bottom loop

5 Keep wrapping the working cord around the other cords, working toward the bottom of the loop. When only a little bit of the bottom of the loop is sticking out past the working cord, thread the working cord through the bottom of the loop.

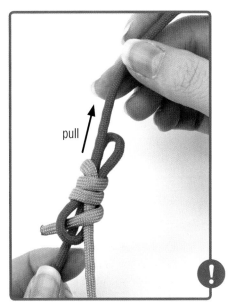

pull

6 Pull on the end of the filler cord at the top of the wrap. This will bring the bottom of the loop and the working cord up against the bottom of the wrap. Trim all the cord ends. Have an adult finish the ends by fusing them or covering them with glue (see page 12). Use the little loop at the top of the wrap to attach a key ring.

COBRA STITCH BRACELET

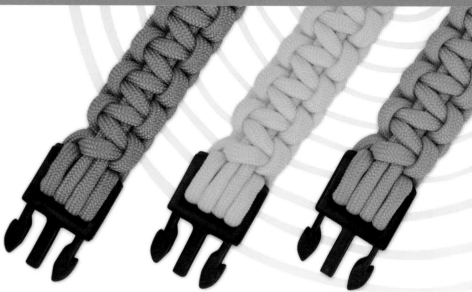

It doesn't get any easier than this! This basic survival bracelet is made using a square knot (also known as a cobra stitch). You'll use this knot a lot, so making this bracelet is a great way to practice. Once you get the hang of it, you'll be making tons of bracelets for you and your friends! When you're ready to change it up, try making a two-color, striped, or charm bracelet.

YOU'LL NEED:

For One-Color Bracelet:

 TURQUOISE
8' (250cm) 550 paracord

 BUCKLE
5/8" (15mm)

For Two-Color Bracelet:

 WHITE
4' (125cm) 550 paracord

 TURQUOISE
4' (125cm) 550 paracord

 BUCKLE
5/8" (15mm)

For Striped Bracelet:

 NEON PINK
8' (250cm) 550 paracord

 WHITE
1' (30cm) 550 paracord

 BUCKLE
5/8" (15mm)

For Regular Charm Bracelet:

 NEON GREEN
8' (250cm) 550 paracord

 SILVER CLOVER CHARM

 BUCKLE
5/8" (15mm)

For Striped Charm Bracelet:

 NEON GREEN
8' (250cm) 550 paracord

 WHITE
1' (30cm) 550 paracord

 SILVER FROG CHARM

 BUCKLE
5/8" (15mm)

KIDS CAN!

Bracelets are great to give as gifts for friends and family, but they're also an awesome way to give back to your community or raise awareness about a cause. Offer to make some bracelets for a church, school, or sports team fundraiser. You can make them in colors to match your cause—like pink and white for breast cancer awareness, or your team's colors for a sports fundraiser. Add motivational beads or other fun charms to make them really stand out. Can you think of some ways you can use your bracelets to impact your community?

ONE-COLOR BRACELET

1 Tie the cord onto a buckle end using a lark's head or double lark's head knot (page 14). Fold the cord in half to form a loop at the center. Feed the cord ends up through a buckle end, then bring the cord ends down through the loop (lark's head). Feed the cord ends up through the buckle and down through the loop again (double lark's head).

2 Bring the cord ends down through the other buckle end. You can wrap each cord around the buckle twice to fill up space. Position the buckle ends so they are about 6½" (16.5cm) apart.

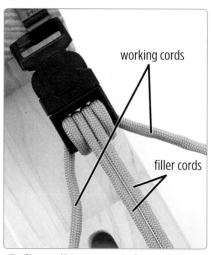

3 There will be two cords that stretch between your buckle ends. These are the filler cords. There will be two loose cords. These are your working cords.

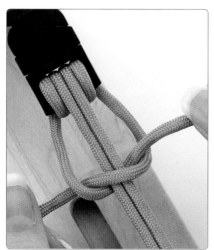

4 Start tying a square knot (page 16). Bring the right working cord over the filler cords. Then bring the left working cord over the right working cord, under the filler cords, and over and through the loop formed by the right working cord. Tighten the knot so it is right next to the buckle.

5 Finish tying the square knot. Bring the left working cord over the filler cords. Then bring the right working cord over the left working cord, under the filler cords, and over and through the loop formed by the left working cord. Tighten the knot.

6 Repeat Steps 4–5 to continue tying square knots (see page 16) until you reach the other buckle end. Then trim the cord ends. Have an adult finish the ends by fusing them or covering them with glue (see page 12).

TWO-COLOR BRACELET

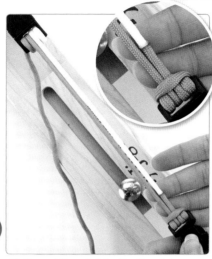

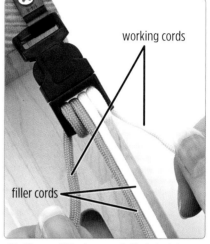

working cords

filler cords

1 To create a two-color bracelet, get an adult's help to fuse two cords together. Ask the adult to follow the steps on page 13 to do this.

2 Repeat Steps 1–2 for the One-Color Bracelet to attach the two-color cord to the buckle ends. You will have to adjust the cord so the place where the two colors are joined is between the buckle ends as shown. Make sure the buckle ends are about 6½" (16.5cm) apart.

3 There will be two cords that stretch between your buckle ends. These are the filler cords. There will be two loose cords. These are your working cords. Your filler cords should be two different colors and your working cords should be two different colors.

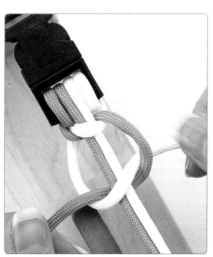

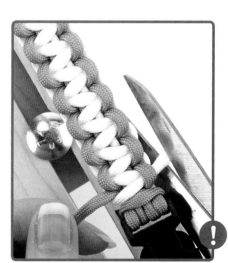

4 Start tying a square knot (page 16). Bring the right working cord over the filler cords. Then bring the left working cord over the right working cord, under the filler cords, and over and through the loop formed by the right working cord. Tighten the knot so it is right next to the end of the buckle.

5 Finish tying the square knot. Bring the left working cord over the filler cords. Then bring the right working cord over the left working cord, under the filler cords, and over and through the loop formed by the left working cord. Tighten the knot.

6 Repeat Steps 4–5 to continue tying square knots (see page 16) until you reach the other buckle end. Then trim the cord ends. Have an adult finish the ends by fusing them or covering them with glue (see page 12).

STRIPED BRACELET

1 Follow the instructions on page 10 to remove the filler from the short cord. Repeat Step 1 for the One-Color Bracelet to attach the long cord to a buckle end using a lark's head knot. Fold the first 2" (5cm) of the stripe cord around the other buckle end. Then, feed the bracelet cords down through that buckle end so the stripe cord is between them. You can wrap each cord around the buckle twice. Make sure the buckle ends are about 6½" (16.5cm) apart.

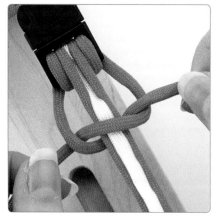

2 Bring the right working cord over the filler and stripe cords. Then bring the left working cord over the right working cord, under the filler and stripe cords, and over and through the loop formed by the right working cord. Tighten the knot so it is right next to the buckle. Make sure the knot goes around the short tail of the stripe cord on the underside of your bracelet.

3 You will tie the next part of the knot under the stripe cord. To do this, flip the stripe cord up out of the way. Then, bring the left working cord over the filler cords. Bring the right working cord over the left working cord, under the filler cords, and over and through the loop formed by the left working cord. Make sure the knot goes around the short tail of the stripe cord.

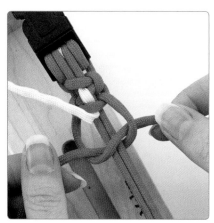

4 Flip the stripe cord back down on top of the filler cords and repeat Step 2 to tie a knot over the filler and stripe cords. Then, repeat Step 3 to tie a knot under the stripe cord as shown. Make sure all of the knots cover the short tail of the stripe cord until you have covered it completely.

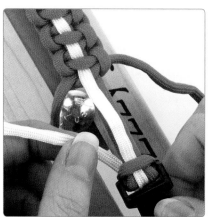

5 Continue repeating Steps 2–3. When you are about 1" (3cm) from the other buckle end, fold the stripe cord around the buckle, feeding it through the loop of the lark's head knot. If you are using a jig, unbuckle the end of the bracelet to make this easier. Continue repeating Steps 2–3 until you reach the buckle. Make sure the knots go around the tail end of the stripe cord.

6 Trim the cord ends, including the tail ends of the stripe cords on the underside of the bracelet if necessary. Have an adult finish the ends by fusing them or covering them with glue (see page 12).

CHARM BRACELET

REGULAR BRACELET

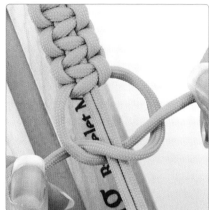

1 Turn to page 22 (the One-Color Cobra Stitch Bracelet) and follow Steps 1–5 until you reach the spot where you would like to add your bead or charm.

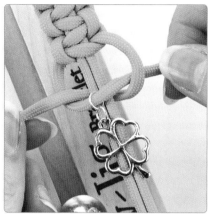

2 When you reach the spot where you would like to add your bead or charm, thread the bead onto the working cord that will cross OVER the filler cords in the next knot (here it is the left cord). Then tie the knot as usual, and position the bead over the center of the bracelet.

3 If using a shoelace charm, continue tying square knots as usual under the charm until you reach the other end. Then, thread the other end of the charm onto the working cord that will cross OVER the filler cords in the next knot (here it is the right cord). Then tie the knot as usual.

STRIPE BRACELET

1 Look at page 24 (the Striped Cobra Stitch Bracelet) and follow Steps 1–4 to tie a square knot stripe pattern until you reach the spot where you would like to add your bead or charm.

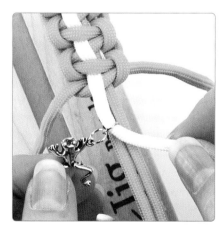

2 When you reach the spot where you would like to add your bead or charm, thread the charm onto the stripe cord when it is flipped up. That way, when you flip the cord down (as shown), the bead will be on top of the bracelet.

3 If using a shoelace charm, continue tying the square knot stripe pattern under the charm until you reach the other end. Then, thread the other end of the charm onto the stripe cord when it is flipped up and continue tying the bracelet.

COBRA COLORS BRACELET

With this design, you can add tons of colors to a basic Cobra Stitch Bracelet! Think of all the fun ways you can mix and match. For a crazy colorful creation, follow Steps 1–3 of the Two-Color Cobra Stitch Bracelet (page 23) to set up a two-color design. Then follow steps 3–10 of this project to add colorful stripes.

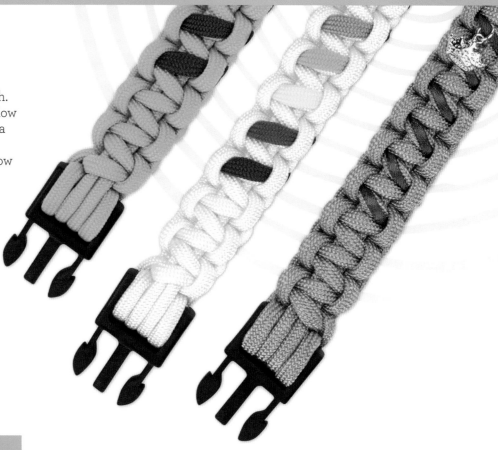

YOU'LL NEED:

For Terrific Turtles:

 NEON GREEN
8' (250cm) 550 paracord

 RED x3
2" (5cm) 550 paracord

 TURQUOISE x2
2" (5cm) 550 paracord

 PURPLE x2
2" (5cm) 550 paracord

 NEON ORANGE x2
2" (5cm) 550 paracord

 BUCKLE
⅝" (15mm)

For Over the Rainbow:

 WHITE
8' (250cm) 550 paracord

 RED x2
2" (5cm) 550 paracord

 NEON ORANGE x2
2" (5cm) 550 paracord

 NEON YELLOW x2
2" (5cm) 550 paracord

 NEON GREEN x2
2" (5cm) 550 paracord

 TURQUOISE
2" (5cm) 550 paracord

 BUCKLE
⅝" (15mm)

For Pretty Princess:

 LIGHT PINK
8' (250cm) 550 paracord

 PURPLE RIBBON x9
2" (5cm) pieces of ⅛" (3mm)-wide ribbon

 SILVER CROWN CHARM

 BUCKLE
⅝" (15mm)

26

1 Remove the filler from your small pieces of paracord (see page 10) and set them aside. Tie the green cord onto a buckle end using a lark's head or double lark's head knot (page 14). Fold the cord in half to form a loop at the center. Feed the cord ends up through a buckle end, then bring the cord ends down through the loop (lark's head). Feed the cord ends up through the buckle and down through the loop again (double lark's head).

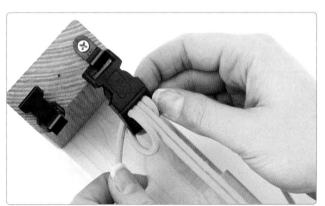

2 Bring the cord ends down through the other buckle end. You can wrap each cord around the buckle twice to fill up the space. Position the buckle ends so they are about 6½" (16.5cm) apart.

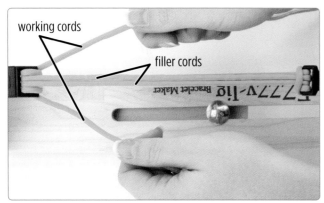

3 There will be two cords that stretch between your buckle ends. These are the filler cords. There will be two loose cords. These are your working cords.

4 Start tying a square knot (page 16). Bring the right working cord over the filler cords. Then bring the left working cord over the right working cord, under the filler cords, and over and through the loop formed by the right working cord. Tighten the knot so it is right next to the end of the buckle.

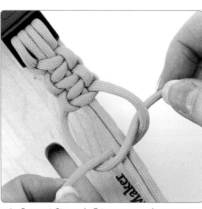

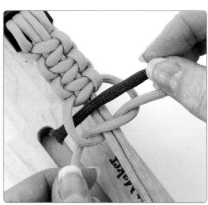

5 Finish tying the square knot. Bring the left working cord over the filler cords. Then bring the right working cord over the left working cord, under the filler cords, and over and through the loop formed by the left working cord. Tighten the knot.

6 Repeat Steps 4–5 two more times so you have tied a total of three square knots. Now let's add the colors!

7 Start tying a square knot by repeating Step 4. As you tighten the knot, you will see a loop forming along the left side of the bracelet. Stick one end of a small red piece of cord through the loop. Finish tightening the knot, making sure the end of the red piece is caught in the loop.

8 Finish tying the square knot by repeating Step 5. As you tighten the knot, you will see a loop forming along the right side of the bracelet. Stick the other end of the red piece of cord through the loop. Finish tightening the knot, making sure the end of the red piece is caught in the loop. Tug on the ends of the red piece at the same time to make sure it is stretched out across the bracelet. You just added your first color!

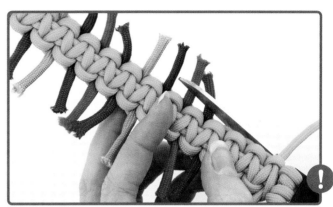

9 Repeat Steps 7–8 to add the remaining small pieces of paracord in this order: blue, purple, orange, red, blue, purple, orange, red. Then, repeat Steps 4–5 three times to tie three square knots. The bracelet should now reach the other buckle end.

10 Flip the bracelet over and trim the ends of all the small paracord pieces as close to the bracelet as possible. Also trim the ends of the working cords. Have an adult finish the ends by fusing them or covering them with glue (see page 12).

OVER THE RAINBOW

To make the Over the Rainbow bracelet, add the small pieces of paracord in this order: red, orange, yellow, green, blue, red, orange, yellow, green.

PRETTY PRINCESS

To make the Pretty Princess bracelet, use ribbon for the color stripes instead of paracord. Cover the ribbon ends with glue to finish them. Thread a bead or charm onto the fifth (center) ribbon before adding it to the bracelet.

FISHTAIL BRACELET

THE KNOT
Fishtail Weave (page 31)

This bracelet is made using a super simple weaving pattern: around, over, down. Once you get the hang of the pattern, you'll be finished in a flash! The two-color version is just a bit more complicated than the one-color version, so try practicing with the one-color bracelet first.

Don't keep it a secret!

YOU'LL NEED:

For Rockstar Red:

 RED
8' (250cm) 550 paracord

 BUCKLE
⅝" (15mm)

For Fun in the Sun:

NEON GREEN
6' (200cm) 550 paracord

NEON YELLOW
6' (200cm) 550 paracord

BUCKLE
⅝" (15mm)

For Super Charm:

 NEON PINK
6' (200cm) 550 paracord

 WHITE
6' (200cm) 550 paracord

 x20 SILVER CHARMS

 BUCKLE
⅝" (15mm)

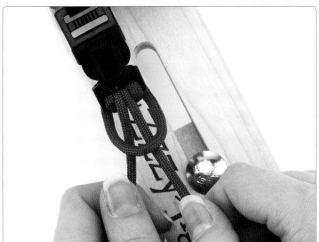

1 Tie the cord onto a buckle end using a lark's head or double lark's head knot (page 14). Fold the cord in half to form a loop at the center. Feed the cord ends up through a buckle end, then bring the cord ends down through the loop (lark's head). Feed the cord ends up through the buckle and down through the loop again (double lark's head).

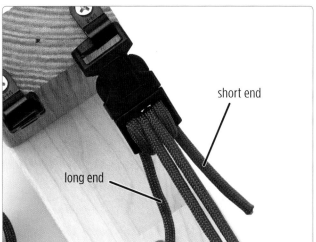

short end

long end

2 Bring the cord ends down through the other buckle end. You can wrap each cord around the buckle twice to fill up the space. Position the buckle ends so they are about 6½" (16.5cm) apart. Now, adjust the cord so one end is very long and the other is very short. The short end should be about 2" (5cm) long.

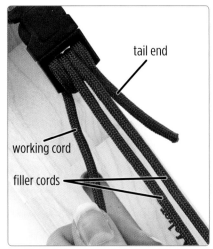

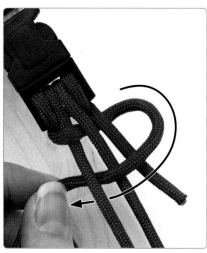

3 There will be two cords that stretch between your buckle ends. These are the filler cords. There will be one long loose cord. This is your working cord.

4 Bring the working cord out to the side of the bracelet (whichever side it is closest to; here it is the left side). Wrap it around and over the left filler cord and feed it down between the two filler cords.

5 Bring the working cord under the right filler cord (and the short tail end) and out to the right side of the bracelet. Wrap it around and over the right filler cord (and the short tail end) and feed it down between the two filler cords.

FUN IN THE SUN

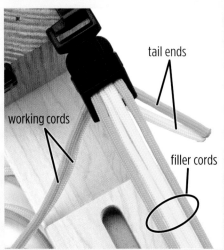

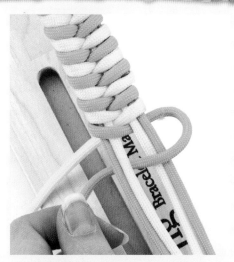

For the Fun in the Sun bracelet, take the two cords and hold them together like they are one cord. Repeat Step 1 to attach the cords to a buckle end, using a lark's head knot instead of a double lark's head knot. Repeat Step 2 to attach the cords to the other buckle end. You will only be able to wrap the cords around the buckle once. You will have four filler cords, two short ends, and two long working cords.

Bring the working cords out to the side of the bracelet (whichever side is closest; here it is the left). Take the farthest left cord (here it is green), wrap it around and over the two left filler cords and feed it down between the four filler cords. Bring the working cord under the two right filler cords and out to the right side of the bracelet. Wrap it around and over the right filler cords (and the short tail ends) and feed it down between the four filler cords. Repeat with the second working cord as shown here.

Continue the fishtail weave, alternating between the green and yellow working cords. Look back to Steps 4–5 if you need help. Repeat Steps 7–8 to finish the bracelet.

6 Repeat Steps 4–5 to continue the fishtail weave. Remember to wrap the working cord around the short tail of the right filler cord until it is completely covered. Continue until you reach the other buckle end.

7 Flip the bracelet over so you are looking at the underside. Loosen the last loop at the end of the bracelet, and feed the working cord through it. Tighten the loop down over the working end of the cord.

8 Trim the end of the working cord. Have an adult finish the end by fusing it or covering it with glue (see page 12).

SUPER CHARM

For the Super Charm bracelet, thread charms onto the working cord as you make the fishtail weave. You can add charms on just one side of the bracelet or on both sides. It's up to you!

TOTALLY TRIPLE BRACELET

THE KNOT
Triple Weave (page 35)

If you're looking for a challenge, this bracelet is for you! It uses a weaving pattern like the Fishtail Bracelet, but the extra width makes it a bit more difficult. Follow each step carefully and compare your project to the pictures as you go to make sure you are weaving the cords correctly. When you're finished, you'll have an awesome cuff bracelet to show off to your family and friends!

YOU'LL NEED:

For Superhero Style:

 RED
5½' (175cm) 550 paracord

 TURQUOISE
5½' (175cm) 550 paracord

 BUCKLE
⅝" (15mm)

For Camo Crazy:

 PINK CAMO
11' (350cm) 550 paracord

 BUCKLE
⅝" (15mm)

For Go Team!:

 YELLOW
5½' (175m) 550 paracord

 PURPLE
5½' (175m) 550 paracord

 SHOELACE CHARM

 BUCKLE
⅝" (15mm)

POW! BOOM! ZAP!

1 To create a two-color bracelet, get an adult's help to fuse two cords together. Ask the adult to follow the steps on page 13 to do this.

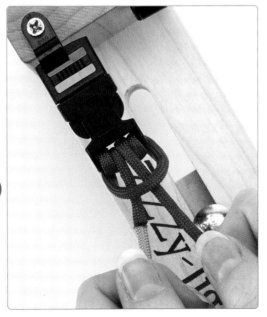

2 Tie the cord onto a buckle end using a lark's head or double lark's head knot (page 14). Fold the cord in half to form a loop at the center. Feed the cord ends up through a buckle end, then bring the cord ends down through the loop (lark's head). Feed the cord ends up through the buckle and down through the loop again (double lark's head).

3 Bring the cord ends down through the other buckle end. You can wrap each cord around the buckle twice to fill up the space. Position the buckle ends so they are about 6½" (16.5cm) apart.

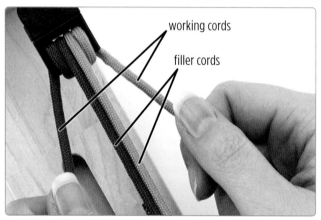

working cords

filler cords

4 There will be two cords that stretch between your buckle ends. These are the filler cords. There will be two loose cords. These are your working cords.

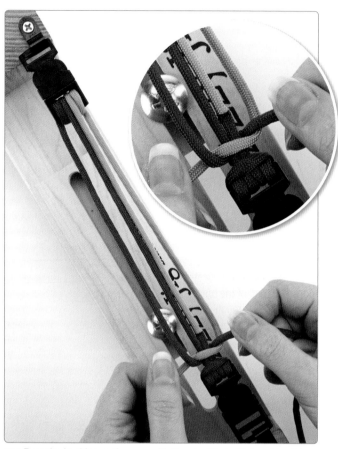

5 Turn the buckles so the one with the double lark's head knot is closest to you. Bring the working cords back to this buckle. Bring the right working cord over the filler cords. Bring the left working cord over the right working cord, under the filler cords, and over and through the loop formed by the right working cord. Tighten the knot just a little so it is against the double lark's head knot. Don't pull the knot too tight, or it will slide down the filler cords toward the other buckle.

6 Now you have four filler cords and two working cords. Take the right working cord and wrap it around the right filler cord. Take the left working cord and bring it around and over the left filler cord, under the two middle filler cords, and over the right filler cord.

7 Take the right working cord and bring it over the two middle filler cords and under the left filler cord. See how the right working cord starts behind the left working cord on the right side of the bracelet and then jumps in front of it on the left side of the bracelet?

8 Repeat Steps 6–7 to continue the triple weave. Continue until you reach the other buckle end.

9 Flip the bracelet over so you are looking at the underside. Loosen the last center loop at the end of the bracelet, and feed the working cords through it. Tighten the loop down over the working ends of the cords.

CAMO CRAZY

To create a one-color bracelet, you will have to use 11' (350cm) of paracord. Skip Step 1 and follow Steps 2–10 to create the bracelet. It's easier to learn the weave for this project using two colors, so practice making a bracelet that way first before you try this variation.

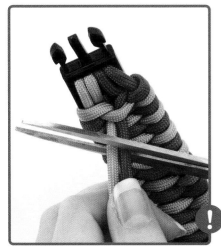

10 Trim the ends of the working cords. Have an adult finish the ends by fusing them or covering them with glue (see page 12).

GO TEAM!

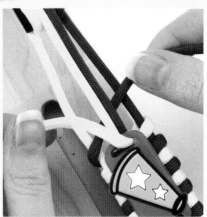

To add a shoelace charm, thread one end of the charm onto the right working cord when you are weaving it over the two middle cords. Continue the triple weave under the charm as usual until you reach the other end.

Thread the other end of the charm onto the right working cord when you are weaving it over the two middle cords, just like you did with the first end. Continue the triple weave after the charm to finish the bracelet.

LOOPY LANYARD OR NECKLACE

THE KNOT
Round Braid (page 18)

Wear this braided project as a sporty lanyard or a stylish necklace—the choice is yours! It's made to be adjustable, so you can make it as long or short as you want. There are loads of things you can attach to the end: keys, a whistle, beads, or a mini-flashlight. What else can you think of?

BREAK TIME!
If you have to stop in the middle of braiding, use binder clips to hold your cords in place until you're ready to start again!

YOU'LL NEED:

For Sportsman's Lanyard:

 BLACK
8' (250cm) 550 paracord

 TITANIUM
8' (250cm) 550 paracord

 KEY RING
1" (25mm)

For Fashionista Necklace:

 x2 **NEON PINK**
8' (250cm) 550 paracord

 RING
⅝" (15mm) solid ring, split ring, or jump ring

 BEADS OR PENDANT
(your choice)

 JUMP RINGS

 JEWELRY PLIERS

38

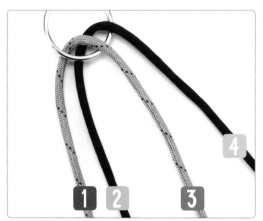

1 This project is made using a round braid (page 18). To start the braid, fold the two cords in half over the key ring. Position the strands so the colors alternate.

2 Bring the far left strand under the two strands in the middle and then back over one to the left. Shown here, the far left gray strand (1) goes under the black and gray strands (2 and 3) in the middle. Then it goes back over the gray strand (3) to the left.

3 Bring the far right strand under the two strands in the middle and then back over one to the right. Shown here, the far right black strand (4) goes under the two gray strands (3 and 1) in the middle. Then it goes back over the gray strand (1) to the right.

4 Repeat Steps 2–3 until the braid is about 2½' (75cm) long. Make sure the braid is long enough to fit over your head comfortably when you make it into a loop.

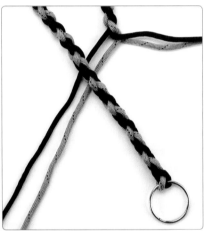

5 Take the end of the braid you are working on and position it a few inches above the key ring. Place the two left working cords behind the braid.

6 Use the working cords to start tying a square knot over the braid. Treat each pair of working cords as one as you tie the knot. Bring the two right working cords over the braid. Bring the two left working cords over the right working cords, under the braid, and over and through the loop formed by the right working cords. Tighten the knot, but do not make it as tight as usual.

7 Try to pull the braid through the knot. It should be a little tough, but not impossible. If you can't pull the braid through the knot, loosen the knot a little until you can.

8 Finish the square knot by bringing the left working strands over the braid. Then bring the right working strands over the left working strands, under the braid, and over and through the loop formed by the left working strands. Tighten the knot, but do not make it too tight.

9 Repeat Step 7 to make sure the braid can slide through the knot. Adjust the knot as needed to make sure the braid can slide through it. This makes the lanyard adjustable!

10 Repeat Steps 6–9 to tie one more square knot over the braid. Make sure the braid can slide through the knot. Trim the ends of the working cords. Have an adult finish the ends by fusing them or covering them with glue (see page 12).

FASHIONISTA NECKLACE

For the Fashionista Necklace, start the braid with a solid ⅝" (15mm) ring instead of a key ring. You can also use a jump ring or split ring. Check the jewelry section of your local craft store for some different options.

Use two cords in the same color to make the braid. Or use two colors—it's up to you! Repeat Steps 1–10 to make the necklace. To add beads, get an adult's help and use jump rings and jewelry pliers to attach a pendant or lots of small beads to the starting ring.

ROCKIN' WRAPS

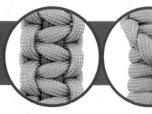

Wraps are a cool way to accessorize all kinds of things...headbands, headphones, water bottles, flashlights, pens and pencils, even your bike! This project will show you how to make two different wraps. The square knot wrap is great for wrapping flat objects, like a wide headband or headphones. The half hitch wrap works best with tube-shaped objects, like a thin headband or a pencil.

YOU'LL NEED:

For Sizzlin' Square Knot Headband:

 NEON PINK
16' (500cm) 550 paracord

 WIDE BLACK HEADBAND

For Totally Twisted Half Hitch Headband:

 NEON PINK
12' (375cm) 325 paracord

 THIN HEADBAND
(any color)

For Stylin' Square Knot Headphones:

 TITANIUM
16' (500cm) 550 paracord

 RETRO HEADPHONES

For Study Buddy Half Hitch Pencil:

 NEON PINK
5' (150cm) 325 paracord

 COLORFUL PENCIL

TIP

Have some extra cord on hand when you start this project. You might need more cord depending on the item you're wrapping. For small items like pens or pencils, you'll need less cord, while large items like flashlights and water bottles will need more cord.

SIZZLIN' SQUARE KNOT HEADBAND

1 Usually a square knot is made over filler cords. When you use a square knot as a wrap, the item you are wrapping becomes the filler! To start, fold your cord in half to find the center point. Place the center of the cord behind the headband, about 1½" (4cm) from one end.

2 Start tying the square knot (see page 16). Bring the right working cord over the headband. Bring the left working cord over the right working cord, under the headband, and over and through the loop formed by the right working cord.

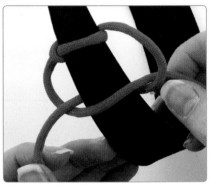

3 Finish the square knot. Bring the left working cord over the headband. Bring the right working cord over the left working cord, under the headband, and over and through the loop formed by the left working cord.

4 Repeat Steps 2–3 to continue tying square knots (see page 16) until you are about 1½" (4cm) from the other end of the headband. Trim the cord ends. Have an adult finish the ends by fusing them or covering them with glue (see page 12).

STYLIN' SQUARE KNOT HEADPHONES

You can wrap lots of things, even headphones! If you have adjustable headphones, make sure you open them up so they are the largest size possible. Wrap each section separately. Don't wrap any of the sections that have to slide back into the headphones to make them smaller.

TOTALLY TWISTED
HALF HITCH HEADBAND

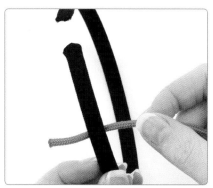

1 This wrap is made using a half hitch as shown on page 15. To start, place one end of your cord under your headband, about 1½" (4cm) from the end. This cord end under your headband is the starting end. The remaining long end is the working end.

2 Bring the long working end of the cord around the short starting end. This will form a loop around the headband. Bring the working end through this loop.

3 You'll make your next knot under the first one. Bring the working end around the headband and cross it underneath itself. This will form a loop around the headband. Tighten the loop.

4 Repeat Step 3, bringing the working end around the headband and crossing it underneath itself. Continue until you reach the other side of the headband, stopping about 1½" (4cm) from the end.

5 Trim both the starting and working cord ends. Have an adult finish the ends by fusing them or covering them with glue (see page 12).

STUDY BUDDY HALF HITCH PENCIL

This wrap is fun to add to all kinds of thin round items, like pencils and pens! If you're feeling really ambitious, try wrapping your favorite sports water bottle or parts of your bike!

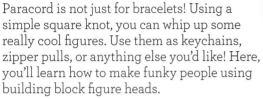

Paracord is not just for bracelets! Using a simple square knot, you can whip up some really cool figures. Use them as keychains, zipper pulls, or anything else you'd like! Here, you'll learn how to make funky people using building block figure heads.

YOU'LL NEED:

⬭ **TURQUOISE**
3' (100cm) 95 paracord

▢ **TOY HEAD**
from a building block figure

◼ **HAMMER**

◼ **SMALL SCREWDRIVER**

1 Get an adult's help to hollow out your building block figure's head with a hammer and screwdriver.

2 Fold the cord in half to form a loop at the center. Feed the loop through the figure head from the top. A rubber band or paper clip can be very helpful for this step. Feed the rubber band or paperclip halfway through the figure head first. Then fold cord in half over the band or clip. Use the band or clip to pull the cord through the figure head.

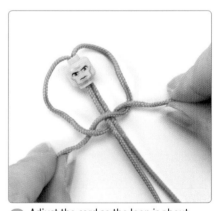

3 Adjust the cord so the loop is about 5" (12.5cm) long. Fold the loose ends down along each side of the figure head. These are the working cords. Start tying a square knot (see page 16). Bring the right working cord over the loop. Bring the left working cord over the right working cord, under the loop, and over and through the loop formed by the right working cord.

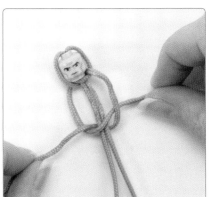

4 Finish the square knot. Bring the left working cord over the loop. Bring the right working cord over the left working cord, under the loop, and over and through the loop formed by the left working cord.

5 Repeat Steps 3–4 three times so you have tied four square knots total. Then turn the figure so the head is closest to you. Repeat Steps 3–4 twice to tie two square knots over the original four square knots you already tied. Repeat Step 3 one more time to tie the first half of a square knot over the original four square knots you already tied.

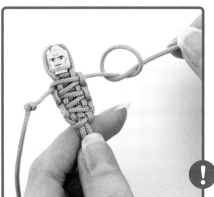

6 The cord ends will form the arms of your figure. Tie a small knot in each cord about ½" (1.5cm) from the body of the figure. Trim the cord ends close to the knots. Have an adult finish the ends by fusing them or covering them with glue (see page 12).

These dainty dragonflies make adorable accessories! They can be attached to anything you want—purses, bags, backpacks, and more. Play around with the sizes of the wings to get different looks, or try using some really funky beads for the eyes!

YOU'LL NEED:

PURPLE
5' (150cm) 550 paracord

x2 **YELLOW PONY BEADS**
(available at your local craft store)

KEY RING
1" (25mm)

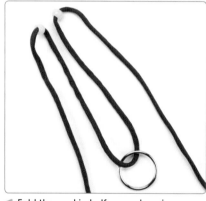

1 Fold the cord in half over a key ring. Thread a pony bead onto each cord end, positioning them about 5" (12.5cm) from the key ring. Fold the cord ends back toward the key ring.

2 Start tying the square knot (see page 16). Bring the right working cord over the filler cords. Bring the left working cord over the right working cord, under the filler cords, and over and through the loop formed by the right working cord. Adjust the beads as you tighten the knot to keep them at the top.

3 Finish the square knot. Bring the left working cord over the filler cords. Bring the right working cord over the left working cord, under the filler cords, and over and through the loop formed by the left working cord.

4 Repeat Step 2. Keep this knot very loose, making even loops on each side of the dragonfly. This will be the first set of wings.

48